Month

Psalm 46:10 *"Be still, and know that I am God."*

There are times in life when God is asking us to be still and know that He is God and that He is able to do what needs to be done in our lives. It's in those still times that God is able to do all that He has promised. It's in your stillness that God is able to move. Will you be still today and allow God to be God in your situation?

My Thoughts:

Month:_____

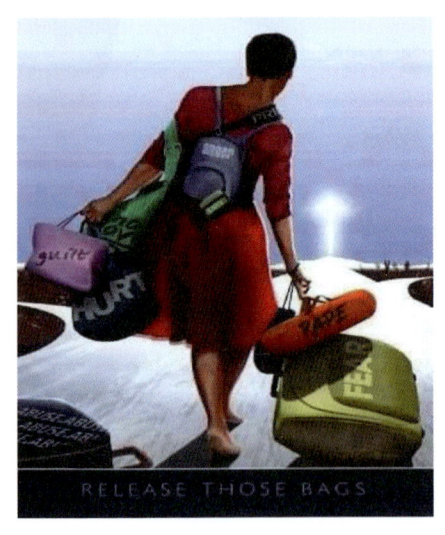

Date:_____

Letting Go of Unnecessary Baggage!

Exodus 14:13 "Do not be afraid. Stand firm and you will see the deliverance the Lord will bring you today."

Sometimes in life we hold on to past stuff that we should let go. We start looking back wanting those things that we have left behind. When god delivers us from our past, let the past stay the past and Leave Your Baggage Behind. What will you let go of today so that you can move forward into all that God has promised you?

My Thoughts:

Month: _____

Date: _____

The Unveiling: No More Masks!

<u>2 Corinthians 3:18</u> "And we, who with unveiled faces all reflect the Lord's glory, are being transformed into his likeness with ever increasing glory, which comes from the Lord, who is the Spirit."

The wounds of your past have scarred you and the pain of your now has obstructed you from becoming and being. You have veiled yourself in a cloak of shame, bitterness, loneliness, rejection and low self-esteem but I have come to break the iron from your hearts and unveil the beauty of Me, says the Lord. What masks do you need to remove so that you can become who God has ordained you to be?

My Thoughts:

Month: _____

Date: _____

Like the Dew in the Morning...Gentle Rest upon My Heart!

Zechariah 8:12 "The seed will grow well, the vine will yield its fruit, the ground will produce its crops, and the heavens will drop their dew."

So many times God gives us "gifts" using the most simple delivery systems known. If we didn't recognize it ourselves or don't have a Moses to point it out to us we would just walk right over, under, around, or through the gift without knowing it. This "manna" delivered in "the dew of heaven" can be the very thing that will be the bread of life that we need to make it through the problem or experience we're facing right now.

My Thoughts:

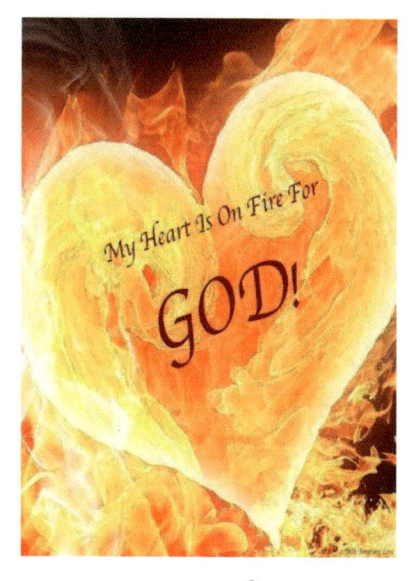

Month: _____

Date: _____

A Heart on Fire for God!

<u>Psalms 51:10</u> "Create in me a pure heart, O God, and renew a steadfast spirit within me."

To cultivate and maintain a heart on fire for God requires regular intake of the Word, an attitude of praise, worship and thanksgiving, purity of heart, body and mind, service to others and a sense of commitment to glorify God and finish the race. A heart on fire creates love: for God and for our fellow human beings.

My Thoughts:

Month:_____

Date: _____

God Has the Last Word!

Proverbs 16:1 "The plans of the heart belong to man, But the answer of the tongue is from the Lord."

You may feel like you've wasted years in a relationship that didn't work out, or years on a job that turned out to be a dead end, but be encouraged today because God is a restorer, a redeemer! Today take a step of faith and believe that for every opportunity you've missed, every chance you've blown, God will make up the difference.

My Thoughts:

Month: _____

Date: _____

The Power of a Godly Woman!

<u>Proverbs 31:30</u> "Favor is deceitful, and beauty is vain: but a woman that fears the Lord, she shall be praised."

The woman's place of submission is a place of power. The woman's role of servant is the role of the Master. The woman's physical weakness is the trait of strength. The woman's lower position is the position of greatness. Is there any reason to desire anything else? Is there any reason to covet the man's place? Why not be grateful for what the Lord has given you and ask Him to maximize its use? Be the godly woman the Lord intended you to be.

My Thoughts:

Month: _____

Date: _____

Fabulous When Victory Comes!

Jeremiah 29:11 "For I know the plans I have for you," declares the Lord, "plans to prosper you and not to harm you, plans to give you hope and a future."

I am a woman of God. I am who God says I am and nothing or nobody can change that. He created me for greatness and I shall become what He has ordained me to be. Trials and tribulations are a part of life but I declare that when my victory comes I shall be fabulous. I am loved by God so much that He has given me predestined life with plans to prosper me and not to harm me, to give me hope and a future. I will be fabulous when my victory comes!

My Thoughts:

Month: _____

Date: _____

The Power of a Praying Woman!

Psalm 6:9 "The Lord has heard my plea; the Lord will answer my prayer."

A woman praying to God is a form of communication where amazing things can happen. Prayer brings us closer to God when we openly come to Him, when we let our guard down, and allow Him into our hearts. Through prayer God can bring healing to the emotionally and physically weak. There is power in prayer and the praying woman!

My Thoughts:

Month: _____

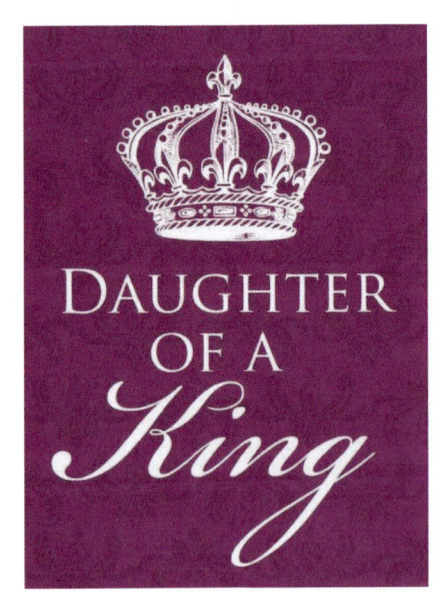

Date: _____

You are The Daughter of a King!

Psalms 139:14 "I will praise You, for I am fearfully and wonderfully made; Marvelous are Your works."

Because God is involved in every woman's life, this makes every woman special from the very beginning. God doesn't make mistakes, you are an original masterpiece of your Creator, and created for a specific purpose! You are the Daughter of the King of Kings...You are Royalty!

My Thoughts:

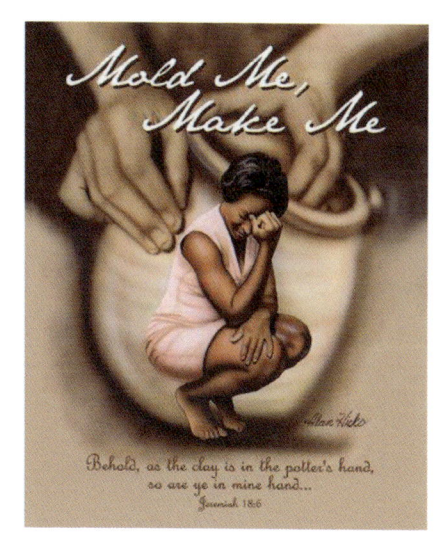

Month: _____

Date: _____

A Broken Woman!

Psalm 34:18 "The Lord is close to the brokenhearted and saves those who are crushed in spirit."

God says "I will carry burdens." If you are lonely, God says "I will never leave you nor forsake you." If you are in need, Jesus will be there for you. Jesus didn't say that we would never walk through difficulties, trials or storms; He did promise us, however, that He would walk beside us and even carry us through those difficult times. Believe that and trust Him!

My Thoughts:

Month: _____

Date: _____

Sugar Coating!

<u>John 8:31-32</u> "If you hold to my teaching, you are really my disciples. Then you will know the truth, and the truth will set you free."

The Bible is a book of truth and thus "All Scripture is God-breathed and is useful for teaching, rebuking, correcting and training in righteousness. The truth should never be sugar coated!

My Thoughts:

Month: _____

Date: _____

Someone Else's Grass!

Exodus 20:17 "Do not covet your neighbor's house"

In today's age we see many who are desperately trying to emulate those who have it all. Fighting their way into debt without any idea or preconception of where they are headed or their demise. They are so focused on someone else's luscious grass that they forget about their own lawn. Keep your eyes on your life and your family!

My Thoughts:

Month: _____

Date: _____

Woman...Created to Soar!

<u>Isaiah 40:31</u> "But they that wait upon the Lord shall renew their strength; they shall mount up with wings as eagles; they shall run, and not be weary; and they shall walk and not faint."

Unshackle yourself from your earthly bonds, spread your wings and go forth into a life of unbridled freedom in Christ! He is the wind underneath your wings!

My Thoughts:

Month: _____

Date: _____

Enjoy the Fruit of Your Labor!

Proverbs 11:30 "The fruit of the righteous is a tree of life, and he who wins souls is wise."

If God took time off to enjoy the fruit of His labor, why then are you on the never ceasing wheel of toil and trouble. Take time to balance your life and learn to truly enjoy the fruit of your labor. Do not envy and chase after the wind. Take time to rest!

My Thoughts:

Month: _____

Date: _____

The Highway of Life!

Isaiah 40:3 "A voice of one calling: In the wilderness prepare the way for the Lord; make straight in the desert a highway for our God."

In life there are times when you move forward on your own peaceful lane while depths of your senses register the lights of distant trials, loss, and grief, but you're so wrapped up in your way of life that you don't recognize the lights of heartache testing your faith until they are upon you. Remove the obstacles in your lane of life and allow yourself a straight drive to Jesus!

My Thoughts:

Month: _____

Date: _____

Seek the Lord!

Isaiah 55:6 "Seek the Lord while he may be found; call on him while he is near"

The eyes of the Lord are everywhere. He is searching to and fro to see if anyone is seeking and trying to remain true to Him. Don't sleep walk through life, but remain faithful, awake and vigilant under the care of the Lord so that you may be in ready in all seasons.

My Thoughts:

Month: _____

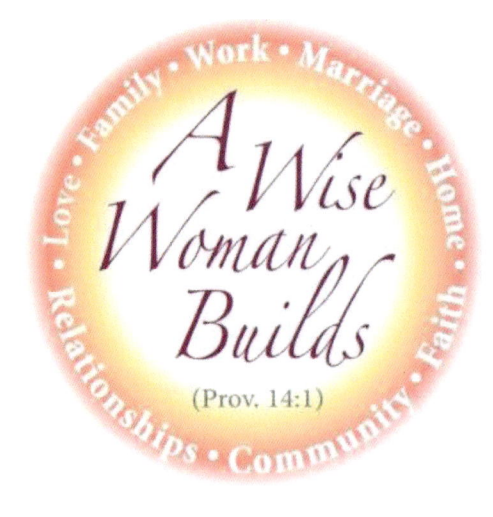

Date: _____

A Wise Woman Builds!

Proverbs 14:1 "A wise woman builds her house, but with her own hands the foolish one tears hers down."

The many qualities of the Virtues woman in Proverbs 31 is an example of a woman who possesses the ability to maintain a home, a business and is resourceful in all matters of her life. She is intelligent, industrious, enterprising, joyful, a homemaker, responsible and uncompromising. She is also hardworking, a lover and a visionary. Guess what…you too have been given these great qualities!

My Thoughts:

Month: _____

Date: _____

Depression…No More!

<u>Psalm 43:5:</u> "Why am I so discouraged? Why so sad? I will put my hope in God! I will praise him again, My Savior and my God."

Depression can be relieved by meditating on God's word. One remedy for depression is to meditate on the record of God's goodness to His people. This will take your mind and focus off your present situation and give you hope that it will improve. How? ....by allowing your thoughts to be focused on God's ability to help you, rather than on your own inability to help yourself.

My Thoughts:

Month: _____

Date: _____

Put Your Trust in God!

Proverbs 3:5-6 "Trust in the Lord with all your heart and lean not on your own understanding; in all your ways acknowledge him, and he will make your paths straight."

Desperately wanting to trust, you begin to trust in and chase after anything and anyone who will make you feel better; but what about God? Can you trust Him? Of course!! Out of all the things in life that will hurt you, despise you, or demean you…God is not one of them. Thank you Lord!

My Thoughts:

Month: _____

Date: _____

An Encounter with God… Choose a Seat!

Revelation 3:20 "Here I am! I stand at the door and knock. If anyone hears my voice and opens the door, I will come in and eat with him and he with me."

Through Jesus Christ we now have the ability to have an encounter with God, Himself…without anyone else being the middle man. He is not interested in how much you make or what, if any possession you own. You don't have to get all dolled up. Your past will not hinder His first impression of you. It doesn't matter what you have done. He will meet you where you are… Choose your Seat!

My Thoughts:

Month: _____

Date: _____

It's Up to You!

Matthew 16:19 "I will give unto thee the keys of the kingdom of heaven: and whatsoever thou shalt bind on earth shall be bound in heaven: and whatsoever thou shalt loose on earth shall be loosed in heaven."

You may be thinking, how or where do we find the nourishment to even consider exploring all the multiple benefits to live life in Balance, Harmony, with Strength and Love and in Christ? Yes, as in most situations, the where is staring us in the mirror, it begins with us! The how is beginning to believe again just how amazing, spectacular and lovely that person staring back in the mirror is! Loose Positivity while binding Negativity and Walk into the promises of God!

My Thoughts:

Month: _____

Date: _____

The Pursuit of Peace!

Psalm 34:14 "Turn from evil and do good; seek peace and pursue it."

Pursuit is the proof of Desire… If you really want something you spend time in the pursuit of it. You know the importance of a thing by the time you're willing to give to it.

My Thoughts:

Month: _____

Date: _____

I Will Give You Rest!

Matthew 11:28
"Come unto me, all ye that labor and are heavy laden, and I will give you rest."

When you finally know you are in Christ, you become satisfied. The troubles of life will go on. The marriage problems may still occur, your job might not last, your health can go and your car may not start – But you have Him! Things come and go in life, but "Jesus Christ is the same yesterday, today, and forever" He who loves you is with you – forever!

My Thoughts:

Month: _____

Date: _____

Lord, Thank You for the Journey!

<u>2 Corinthians 2:15</u> "For we are unto God a sweet fragrance of Christ, in them that are saved, and in them that perish:"

As women of God we must learn how to give thanks in all things. Thank you for the journey Lord….I haven't made it to my destined place yet but I thank you for the wilderness experience…I thank you for my journey!

My Thoughts:

Month: _____

Date: _____

The Blessings of the Lord!

<u>Proverbs 10:22</u> "The blessings of the Lord, it maketh rich, and He addeth no sorrow with it."

Every promise of God is, Yes and Amen in Christ Jesus. When we act on those promises and believe that our actions released the blessing of increase that is in them, then they are Yes and Amen in us. It is done!

My Thoughts:

Month: _____

Date: _____

Dance by Faith until Your Victory Comes!

Psalm 150:4 "*Praise him with the timbrel and dance.*"

Women of God….Dance on the devil's head, Dance on his hands and feet and don't you stop dancing until your victory comes. By faith pick up your spiritual feet and Dance, Dance, Dance until your victory comes!

My Thoughts:

Patty Lee Ministries

It is my sincere hope and prayer that this year will be one of the best years you've ever had. I decree blessings to fall upon God's people like the dew in the morning. I decree the word of God that no weapon formed against you shall prosper and every tongue that rises against thee in judgment thou shalt condemn. I declare that you shall be the head and not the tail in every situation and blessed coming in and blessed going out in every circumstance. I believe that God is getting ready to open some doors that no man can close and opening some blinded eyes that didn't see the favor on your life and their turning their no into a yes. I believe that this is your year so get up and claim it...and tell that devil you gonna be mad my feet hit the ground this morning. May God lead you on the path of righteousness while blessing you all the way! Hang in there and Don't Give Up...

You're Gonna Make It!

Yours Truly, Pastor Patty Lee

What things have you learned and changed about yourself while on your journey to a stronger woman of God over the past year?

Notes:

Printed in Great Britain
by Amazon